White Tails And Other White Tales

Written and Illustrated By The Second Grade Students Of Longfellow Elementary In West Allis, Wisconsin

Scholastic Inc. New York Toronto London Auckland Sydney Mexico City New Delhi Hong Kong Buenos Aires

ORIGINAL COVER

W9-AHK-892

Dedicated
to our
Principal
Mrs. Moe

MEET THE AUTHORS

Top, left to right: Ricardo Bush, James Duarte, Sierra Zoboroski-Conn, Kennedy Schultz, Naydia Bates, Frank Duque, Mrs. Wandsneider, Pedro Gaona, Lorena Mercado, Keith Payne, Kaiya Schrank, Hayden Aitken, Mariah Gilbert

Front, left to right: Steve Johns, Ruby Martinez Castaneda, Elana Hernandez-Zaccone, Olivia Frank, Brent Manvilla, Jaiden Barnes

Did you ever see, in the woods or the zoo,
a completely white creature
that really surprised you?

Some poor animals are born without color,
which leaves them unlike any other.

4

With no pigment,
albinos are white and rare,
adapting to a life with
special care.

Amazing albinos are hard to find.
Here are some animal tales of all kinds.

On a eucalyptus tree branch
sits a sleepy koala bear.
This pouched mammal
eats leaves without a care.

7

An albino baby koala hugs her mom tight,
while her white fur stands out in plain sight.

In the deep green woods, lives the white-tailed deer.
This spotted animal blends in with little fear.

An albino deer can blend in with the snow.
Except for his antlers, you'd hardly know!

Besides the green garden, stands a proud peacock.
This colorful bird shows off quite a lot.

A partial albino peacock has no bright colors,
making him boring to all the others.

In the hot Australian sun,
hops a mother kangaroo.
This strong marsupial
carries around a joey, too.

An albino kangaroo
can burn in the sun.
His pale skin
makes desert life no fun.

Inside a garbage can
digs a curious masked raccoon.
This nocturnal hunter
sneaks around under the moon.

15

An albino raccoon has poor eyesight,
which makes hunting hard during the dark night.

Up high in an old pine tree
perches a dark black crow.
This smart animal
can put on a loud show.

An albino crow can't find a mate at all,
even with his echoing caw-caw.

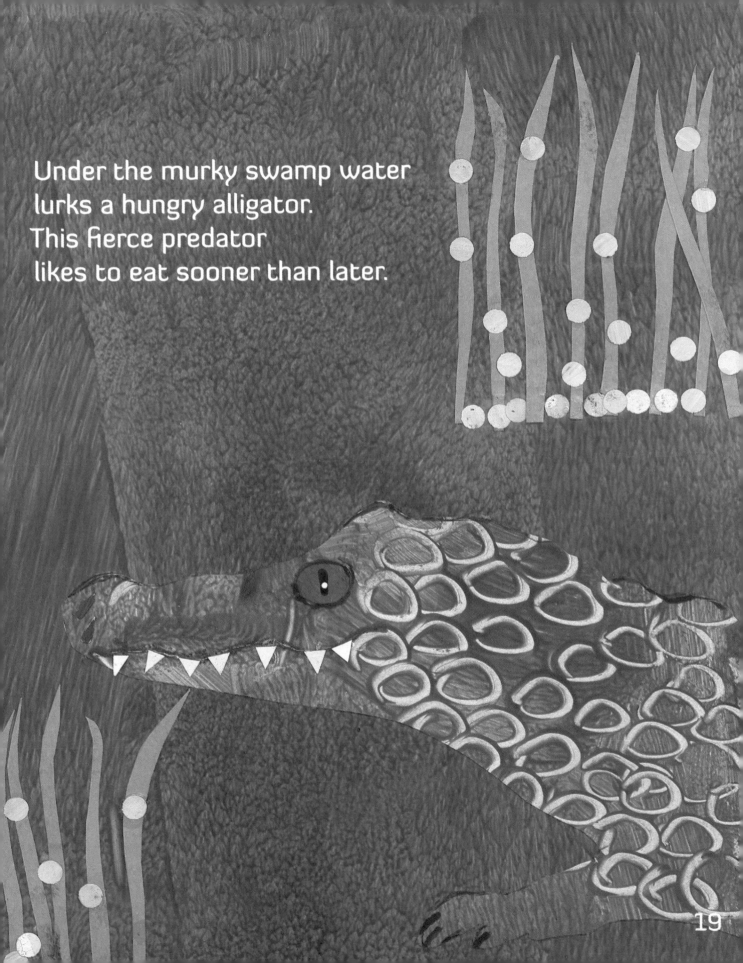

Under the murky swamp water
lurks a hungry alligator.
This fierce predator
likes to eat sooner than later.

19

An albino alligator
cannot hide.
It's hard to catch food
no matter how he tries.

20

On the cool night sand,
crawls a sea turtle just hatched.
This young reptile must hurry
before he gets snatched.

An albino turtle stands out in the dark,
an easy snack for a bird or a shark.

Near an old brown tree
sits a pointy porcupine.
This spiny animal
has quills long and fine.

23

An albino porcupine
is an easy mark,
sitting still and clawing
on rough tree bark.

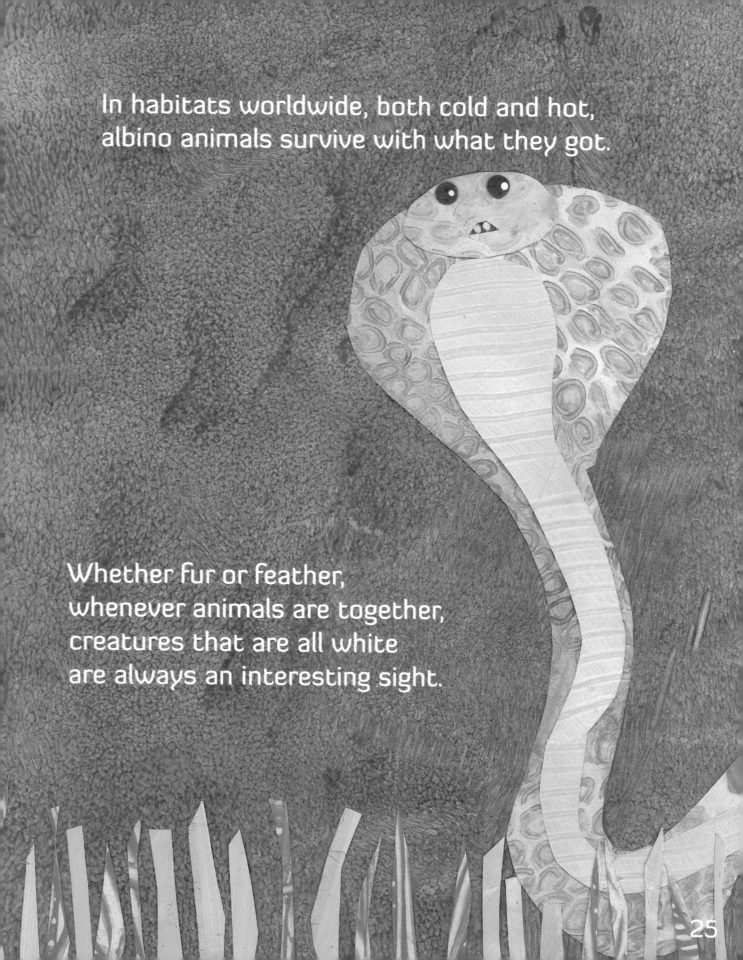

In habitats worldwide, both cold and hot,
albino animals survive with what they got.

Whether fur or feather,
whenever animals are together,
creatures that are all white
are always an interesting sight.

FUN FACTS

Melanin is a pigment that makes color in skin, hair, and eyes.

Albinos are born with no pigment. They have white fur, feathers, scales, or skin.

Not all white animals are albino. Look at the animal's eyes. The eyes are pink, red, or blue.

Cold-blooded albino animals like alligators and snakes need the sun for warmth. But the sun is dangerous to their delicate skin.

Albino snakes and alligators are really rare. There are only about 30 albino alligators that exist.

People can have albino animals, like rabbits, hedgehogs, and hamsters, as pets.

Zookeepers in Australia have to put sunscreen on albino kangaroos.

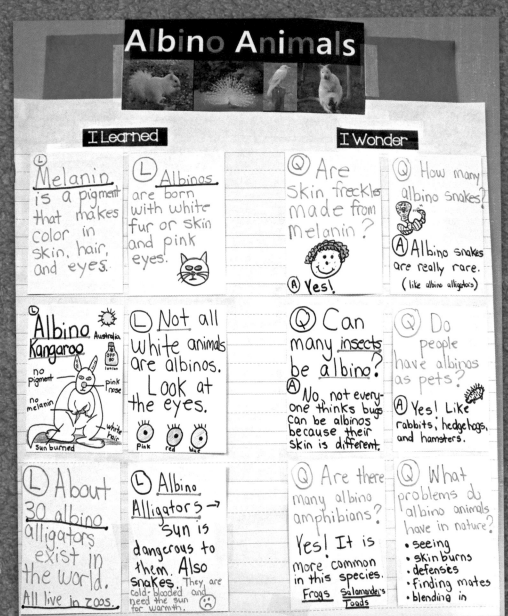

Albino Animals

I Learned

ⓛ Melanin is a pigment that makes color in skin, hair, and eyes.

ⓛ Albinos are born with white fur or skin and pink eyes.

ⓛ Albino Kangaroo — Australia — no pigment — no melanin — pink nose — white hair — sun burned

ⓛ Not all white animals are albinos. Look at the eyes. — pink, red, blue

ⓛ About 30 albino alligators exist in the world. All live in zoos.

ⓛ Albino Alligators → Sun is dangerous to them. Also snakes. They are cold-blooded and need the sun for warmth.

I Wonder

ⓠ Are skin freckles made from melanin? ⓐ Yes!

ⓠ How many albino snakes? ⓐ Albino snakes are really rare. (like albino alligators)

ⓠ Can many insects be albino? ⓐ No, not everyone thinks bugs can be albinos because their skin is different.

ⓠ Do people have albinos as pets? ⓐ Yes! Like rabbits, hedgehogs, and hamsters.

ⓠ Are there many albino amphibians? Yes! It is more common in this species. Frogs Salamanders Toads

ⓠ What problems do albino animals have in nature?
• seeing
• skin burns
• defenses
• finding mates
• blending in

Kids Are Authors®
Books written by children for children

The Kids Are Authors® Competition was established in 1986 to encourage
children to read and to become involved in the creative process of writing.
Since then, thousands of children have written and illustrated books as participants
in the Kids Are Authors® Competition.

The winning books in the annual competition are published by Scholastic Inc.
and are distributed by Scholastic Book Fairs throughout the United States.

For more information:
Kids Are Authors® 1080 Greenwood Blvd., Lake Mary, FL 32746
Or visit our website at: www.scholastic.com/kidsareauthors

ISBN-978-0-545-64594-2
12 11 10 9 8 7 6 5 4 3 2 1

Cover design by Bill Henderson
Printed and bound in the U.S.A.
First Printing, June 2013